Books by Bill Doar

The Magic of Pawleys Island,

Roofs Over My Head,

A Brief History of Georgetown,

A Murder in Georgetown

Letters from Iwo Jima

LETTERS
FROM
IWO JIMA

By
Bill Doar

Letters From Iwo Jima
Copyright © 2015
Bill Doar

ISBN: 978-1-941069-25-7

Clock Tower Books Publishing
Georgetown SC 29440

clocktowerbookspublishing@gmail.com
www.Clocktowerbooksgeorgetown.com

Forward

My father, William Walter (Billy) Doar, was born in Georgetown, S. C. on April 14, 1903 to Elizabeth B. Doar and J. Walter Doar. He died in Georgetown on May 26, 1989 as result of injuries he received in an automobile accident several days earlier. In between these events he lived life to the fullest. He loved the low country of South Carolina around Georgetown, and he hunted the marshes and fished the rivers and Atlantic Ocean throughout his entire life.

In 1935, when I was born, my Dad, Mother and Sister were all living on Kensington Plantation owned by my Grandfather J. Walter Doar. When the last bean crop sold for much less than hoped, Kensington Plantation was lost. Prior to that, Dad had been an aspiring physician, but was forced to drop out of the Medical College of South Carolina as a result of the depression. He was a product of the Great Depression which had a great influence on him.

After the surprise attack on Pearl Harbor on December 7, 1941, he was determined to serve his country, and he did so with distinction.

Letters from Iwo Jima was also a 2006 Japanese-American war movie directed and co-produced by Clint

Eastwood. The film portrays the battle of Iwo Jima from the perspective of the Japanese soldiers' defending the island and is almost entirely in Japanese; although produced by American companies. Eastwood also produced Flags of our Fathers which depicts the same battle from the American view point.

The following letters were handwritten by Dad. Many were written from the war zone off the Pacific Island of Iwo Jima, a Japanese stronghold. Iwo Jima was one of the fiercest battles of World War II.

Dad was a private person so I question whether he would approve of disclosing the contents of these personal letters. However, after reading them, I believe it important to share them since they give wonderful insights into the thoughts, concerns and frustrations of one of many brave men facing a fanatical enemy during World War II.

February 2015 is the 70th anniversary of the assault on Iwo Jima. I know Dad would have liked to have been one of the 30 or more Veterans who returned to the barren Japanese island to observe the ceremonial raising of Old Glory on Mount Suribachi.

Pearl Harbor Day: "a day that will live in infamy." My father was 38 years old. He had fished and hunted the waters around Georgetown for many years; therefore, his choice of military service was the Navy. And there was no question that he was going to serve his country. But because of his age, he literally had to fight his way into the military service. As a member of the Home Guard, it looked as though he would join the Army, but he held out and was ultimately awarded a commission in the Navy as a lieutenant, junior grade. He was delighted. His first assignment was at Opalaka Naval Air Station, Miami, Florida, as a supply officer.

Doar Family, Miami, Florida 1942-1943

However, as plans for an offensive in the Pacific Theatre developed, more ships and trained combat crews would be needed. Sea duty was right up Dad's alley. He spent a short tour at May Port, Florida, near Jacksonville, commanding an aircraft rescue boat retrieving downed airmen, but shortly thereafter, he was transferred to the amphibious training center at Little Creek, Virginia. After graduation he was appointed commanding officer of LSM-60 and promoted to full lieutenant, the same rank as an Army Captain.

Graduation: Crew of LSM 60.

The amphibious invasion of Iwo Jima stemmed from the need for an air base near the Japanese homeland. The island was roughly 575 miles from Japan and was an ideal location for landing fields for crippled B-17s or fighter escorts returning from Japan bombing raids. But as it turned out, Okinawa was even closer to Japan and had better landing fields; therefore, Iwo Jima was used only sparingly. However, Iwo Jima was a stepping stone to the Japanese homeland and was an important battle in the defeat of Japan.

Iwo Jima was defended by approximately 23,000 Japanese army and navy troops. It was attacked by approximately 45,000 Marines organized into three U.S. Marine divisions after months of air and naval bombardment. The Japanese fiercely defended the island from an elaborate network of coves, dugouts, tunnels and underground installations. The island was covered with deep volcanic sands which slowed the movement of tanks, artillery and other heavy equipment. The Japanese decided to stand and fight rather than conduct suicide assaults as they did defending other Pacific islands. Despite the difficulty of the conditions, the U. S. Marines wiped out the defending forces after a month of intense fighting. The Japanese fought to the bitter, hopeless end. American losses included 5,000 killed and 17,400 wounded; however, the entire Japanese garrison was destroyed. The island was declared secure on March 26, 1945 although there remained sporadic fighting thereafter.

On April 12, 1945, President Delano Roosevelt died in Warm Springs, Georgia, and Vice President Harry S. Truman became President on April 30, 1945. Adolph Hitler committed suicide on April 30, 1945 and Germany surrendered on May 7, 1945. The first atomic bomb used in warfare, "Little Boy", was dropped on

Hiroshima, Japan, on August 6, 1945. The second atomic bomb, "Fat Man", was dropped on Nagasaki, Japan, on August 9, 1945, and Japan surrendered unconditionally on August 14, 1945. The surrender ceremony presided over by General Douglas McArthur was held on the Battleship USS Missouri, in Tokyo Bay on September 2, 1945 ending World War II. The two atomic attacks killed hundreds of thousands of Japanese civilians and were the events that convinced the Japanese that the further defense of their homeland was futile. It is estimated that these attacks saved over as many as one million military and civilian lives.

World War I was touted as the war to end all wars. World War II was the war to rid the world of tyrannical dictators. Today, unfortunately, wars seem inevitable, but few in the general public seem engaged. During World Wars I and II, the civilian population was active in the war effort. But today few Americans even know anyone serving in the military.

An LSM was a medium landing ship designed for amphibious landings. The ship loaded with tanks, troops and supplies would drop a stern anchor, proceed to the beach, drop its ramp and offload its cargo, reverse its engines, then pull itself back from the beach against the stern anchor line. The landing was a success unless the ship turned sideways to the beach. That could be costly. The ship would then be a sitting target for enemy artillery.

LSM 60 (center) on its way to Iwo Jima.

Lt. Doar on the ramp of LSM 60 at Iwo Jima.

LSM-60 had an interesting history. It was built in a shipyard in Houston, Texas, and was commissioned on August 25, 1944, after which Dad took command. LSM-60 sailed through the Panama Canal to San Diego,

California where it joined other ships of the fleet. LSM-60 traveled to Pearl Harbor then West across the Pacific Ocean to the beach at Iwo Jima; then back to San Francisco, California, where Dad left the ship and was transferred to Camp Perry near Williamsburg, Virginia. LSM-60 was later de-commissioned and, unceremonially, blown to bits on July 25, 1946 as the platform for an atomic bomb exploded during "Operations Crossroads" Test Baker at Bikini Atoll in the Pacific Ocean.

LSM 60 was used as the platform for the 1946 "Operation Crossroads" atomic bomb test.

The naval assault on Iwo Jima, which in Japanese means sulfur island, began in earnest on February 19, 1945. Iwo Jima was a small island with a dead volcano named Mount Suribachi. I recall Dad telling me that one of the few captured Japanese soldiers commented to his captors that their engineers had tried to build a road to the peak of Mount Suribachi without success; however, the American Marines constructed the road in approximately two weeks. Maybe that is why the Marines were victorious – skill and fortitude. Mount Suribachi was the site of the world famous American flag raising. A statute of that flag raising is a major attraction at Washington, D.C.

Offloading equipment from LSM 60.

My father was a prolific letter writer. Crossing the vast Pacific Ocean between San Diego, California, and Hawaii to Iwo Jima and back left little to do except steer clear of other ships in the convoy, try to sleep, and write letters – and letters he did write.

He not only corresponded with his wife, my mother, Julia, he wrote friends back home. In many of Dad's letters he complained about his lack of sleep and the poor mail service, both understandable problems in a war zone. Although Mother wrote him religiously, delivery of the mail was poor and the mail was usually delivered in bunches. In addition to describing the assault on Iwo Jima, he often inquired about my sister, Amaryllis, me and his Labrador retriever, Wag. He often addressed my Mother as "Sugar", "Honey", "Sweetie", and "Julie" and most of the references to the enemy would not be politically correct today.

On his way to the combat zone, Dad became concerned that he might not return home to his family. Dad wrote a letter to me dated December 29, 1944 and sent it to my Mother. The envelope was addressed to *Wm. Walter Doar, Jr. Not to be opened until his sixteenth birthday.* I was 9 years old on December 29, 1944 and would have been 16 years old on March 9, 1951. Thankfully, Dad was in Georgetown by that time.

Dear Bill:

This is written at a time when the future is very uncertain for me. Uncertain that is as to whether or not I'll come back from an operation against the enemy. It is very certain that I'll be going.

I'm writing this now because I'd like to give you certain advice on your 16th birthday – at the time when you are passing from a child into a man – you will have to start assuming responsibilities. There will be lots of time when you'll have to make decisions to do the right things when it would be lots easier to do the wrong

14

things. Have the courage of your convictions, my son, and do what you know is right.

You were always a good boy, Bill. When I was there, Julia and I taught you what was right and wrong. You had a good start, even for so small a boy and since that time I know that Julia has guided you right.

So now, my young man, you will be assuming your responsibilities.

Don't forget Julia. She is a wonderful woman, Bill, and you are fortunate to have her for a mother. She almost gave her life to bring you into the world and you owe her a debt of gratitude and love which you can never repay – but try to.

Don't forget Amaryllis – She is your sister – closer to you by blood than any person in the world. She is a lovely child. You two were brought up in the "nest" together and almost one of the first words you said was "Amarydis". Protect her and be sweet to her.

Don't forget me, Bill. I am sure that you remember what good times we used to have. As a little baby boy you used to follow me fishing all day long. If the war hadn't of come I'd have taught you to like hunting and fishing as much as I do. I hope you've learned anyway.

My definite advice to you is to go to college. Thru insurance I've provided a sufficient sum to enable you to go. You will not be able to "run around and have a big time" but many a man has gone thru college on less – and I hope you apply yourself and get the most out of your studies. There will be another war so I'd suggest the Citadel. Prepare yourself and whatever else you do keep up with your military so that when you go you will know what to do. War is a grim business.

This country of ours is worth fighting for. That is why I've come thousands of miles from home to fight an enemy that would take it away from us and turn it into a

15

place that would be intolerable to us.

You are from a good family, Bill, on both sides – You are from people who accomplished things, so you will have to live up to these traditions. There will be disappointments and at times things will be discouraging. Those are the times when a man – a real man – stands up and fights and comes out a winner. I know that my son will do that.

I'm sorry that I can't be with you today, Bill. However, what I've written above is the advice I'd give you if I were there. I love you, my son, and I know that you will do what is expected of you – All my love,

Daddy

W. W. Doar
Lieut., USNR,
Commanding Officer

As a child, and because he liked playing "army" and "war" games, Dad was nicknamed, "Solger" (obviously misspelled) by his boyhood friend, Lucas Ford, who grew up on Highmarket Street in Georgetown with Dad. Lucas was always a character, full of jokes and dry wit. As a young adult, he went west to Hilo Hawaii to make his fortune and apparently he did as an insurance executive. Unfortunately, Dad missed meeting Lucas on Dad's short layover in Hawaii on Dad's way out, but after the war they had a glorious reunion in Georgetown.

On January 27, 1945, Lucas Ford wrote Dad:

Dear Solger,

You must have been very close to this island when you passed if you could see the tops of Mauna Loa and Mauna Kea. They are both very beautiful now and last night after coming out of the movie it was beautiful to see the full moon glistening on the snow which had an iridescent glow in the moonlight. Boy it would have made you feel good to have seen it. Sort of cold too at night. Well anyway I sure am disappointed and am counting on you coming here on the return trip so you can see what a place this is. I have everything that you need and a lot of things that are not needed.

See in the Georgetown paper where a Naval lieutenant who was out here with Harold Kaminski, is now visiting him in Georgetown. I knew him well. Sure would like to be there and take him out hunting on Keithfield. And while talking about hunting, it reminds me that in the Georgetown Times was an article about George Vanderbilt being confined to the hospital in Charleston on account of sickness gotten while in command of the PT boat in the South Pacific. That's news to me.

Every now and then I meet a fellow from home. The other day a young fellow who used to be on the Sea Cloud and who married one of the Powell gals, came in and had a long talk with him. His name is Innis and maybe you remember him. He said that he remembered you when you first got in jail.

Am planning to go back home for a year after the war and do nothing except hunt and fish. This reminds me of going down to meet a young man who was coming in on the boat from a two months trip to another island. Was standing by his wife on the dock and they started wigwagging to each other. I noticed that he made the letters FF and she answered with the letters EF. It sounds strange so I asked her what sort of code she used. She told me that EF meant, "Eat First". I was too embarrassed to ask about his code.

Write again Solger, and tell me about your trip.
Sincerely, Lucas

Dad also wrote to his good friend, Sylvan Rosen. Sylvan was Dad's attorney and after the war served as Mayor of Georgetown. Dad served with him as a member of City Council. Sylvan and his brother, Meyer, practiced law in Georgetown for many years and were excellent attorneys.

Other than my Mother and Grandmother, the local who probably wrote Dad the most was Rev. Henry Desassau Bull, the longtime Rector of Prince George, Winyah, Church. I was baptized by Rev. Bull while the Doar family was living at Kensington Plantation.

Rev. Bull was an outstanding person and minister. He became Rector of Prince George Winyah in 1924. He preached at Prince George Winyah Church at 10:00 A.M. on Sunday morning and at All Saints, Waccamaw, Pawleys Island, at 2:00 PM that Sunday afternoon. On Sunday night he drove about 20 miles to Plantersville where he held services at Prince Frederick's Church. Rev. Bull was a busy man. In addition to writing Dad, he sent him a copy of the Church Book of Common Prayer; although I am not certain he ever received it. Rev. Bull left Prince George in early 1953, the year I graduated from Winyah High School, and became Rector of an Episcopal church in Barnwell, S.C.

After being at sea for some time, Dad continued to complain about the mail service. On February 4, 1945 he wrote my mother, Julia, the following letter:

Dear Julie:

When we arrived here yesterday the mail situation looked pretty hopeless. We got the mail which we had written, off on a fuel barge which promised to take it ashore for us. However that didn't give us any mail. Late yesterday afternoon a boat brought us mail. I received four letters from you, one from Dr. Bell and a V-mail from Judge Higgins. Tell them I appreciated them. This P.M. mail was brought to us again but we couldn't get our mail off. I had four letters from you and one from Mamma. I now have yours thru the 26th. That is pretty good for so many thousands of miles away. We will not be here long and I do not believe that this will get in the mail until the next stop but I hope it will.

We had swimming parties both this A.M. and this P.M. The boys all enjoy it so much and it is about the only recreation we have had since the 11th of Jan. I went in the P.M. and it was very refreshing. Several of the boys tried to fish but the water is so deep where we are anchored that the line would not reach bottom.

I'm too sorry that Bill developed mumps but as you say it is best to have them now instead of later.

I have a G.I. haircut. With my mustache off I look like a wrestler and I sure am an ugly cuss. Maybe I can scare the Japs.

I sure hope that Am did not develop them until at least after today so she could be confirmed. I am proud of her.

I think that both of the children had fine reports and certainly hope that Amaryllis has learned her lesson on carelessness. She should know how to <u>prove</u> her answers to she can tell when they are wrong.

Dr. Bell wrote that the two Ford boys were mixed up in the fire alarm ringing with the Bruorton girl but of course innocent.

My crew has been in excellent health I am glad to say. Some of the others have not fared so well. We have plenty of good food and most of us are getting fat. While underway sleep is hard to get enough of and we welcome the several nights' rest that we are able to get while here. Wish I could tell you about this place. Not so very long ago the Japs held it. I have not been able to get ashore and don't believe there is much to go there for.

I love and miss all of you. What wouldn't I give to kiss Amaryllis, spank Bill and hold you close to me. See that Bill gets to hunt and fish whenever there is a chance. I love you. Billy.

Lt. W. W. Doar, USNR

As LSM-60 neared Iwo Jima things turned from routine to excitement. Dad wrote Mother the following letter on February 7, 1945:

Dear Julie:

We've had a little excitement twice in the past 16 hours to break the monotony. Yesterday P.M. we *received word that enemy planes had been seen taking off from one of the nearby islands held by them and were heading in our direction. We went to G. Q. and after waiting about an hour received word that they had turned back. Before sunrise this A.M. word came that enemy surface units were closing in on us. That was bad for anything that would venture out here would surely outgun us. After about 30 minutes they turned out to be <u>our</u> side. That was <u>good</u>. We are spoiling for a fight but at least on something like equal terms.*

The weather is still warm and downright <u>hot</u> from about 1400 to sunset. I've certainly seen enough sunrises and sunsets to last me for a while – <u>everyday</u> – and if you want to see the sunrise when I get back you'll have to look at it by yourself. I'll manage to get up in time to take in the sunsets.

Hope Bill is thru with his mumps and that Amaryllis got by without them. Lots of love to you all.

I love you, Billy

W. W. Doar
Lieut., USNR, Commanding Officer

C.O. Doar at Battle Station.

Dad explained to Mother why he was unable to contact her during his layover in Hawaii in a letter he wrote on February 8, 1945:

In the blue Pacific

Dear Julie:

I will add another chapter to the serial altho there really isn't very much to write about. There has been nothing but the usual routine for the past 24 hours. The weather continues <u>hot</u>. Looked like we would get a little rain but it just spit a few drops and went on off.

I could not phone you from Hawaii because I was attached to a <u>ship</u>. Personnel attached to the base or passing enroute can but no one attached to a ship can phone beyond the limits of the Island. I could not even phone Lucas or wire him or even tell him outright where I was.

I never did go to Honolulu but twice, because there was nothing to go there for. It was terribly crowded with service men and both times I went I had to stand in line for an hour awaiting transportation. I was in several ports but did not get to leave the ship as I was too busy. I saw all of the Islands but one – and they are very beautiful. I got to see the Island of Hawaii – snow-capped Mona Loa and Mona Kea from a distance of 50 miles. That was very pretty. I guess these letters will get in the mail in a day or two and hope that mail will be waiting for us when we get in. I love all of you.

I love you, Billy

On February 11, 1945 Dad wrote to Mother:

Gee Honey:

I'm too sorry about Am having the mumps. I was hoping that she would go until after the 4th before they hit her. Yesterday your letters of the 19, 24 and 27 came and today yours of the 29th. After they brought mail to us they would not take ours. We finally got ours transferred to a larger ship today and they promised to take it ashore when they could. I sure do hope that they will but can't say – I have no idea when this will get in the mail either.

We are anchored way out and not having a power boat have to depend on others, which is no good. They always anchor the LSM's at the end of the world until it comes time to hit the beach.

Tell Bill I've seen a good many B-29's flying around – the first I've seen. They are quite a plane. Yes. Tuesday morning as we were coming in we saw one crash in taking off. It immediately burst into flames and exploded – 12 good men gone to Kingdom Come. Killed by Tojo as surely as if he had pulled the trigger. The dirty yellow bastards ought to be run off the face of the earth – and many of them will be.

I left the ship today for the first time in almost a month. The circumstances were that one of my upper front teeth was aching so bad that the whole left side of my face was aching. The Fifth Officer had one aching in the same place except on the right side. After begging and begging the Medical Officer finally got a boat to come and take us aboard a tender up in the harbor that had a dentist aboard. He took one look and now the Fifth Officer and I are minus an upper tooth. With my hair 1/2 inch "short", minus mustache and front tooth,

I sure am ugly as hell.

Did you read the article in Time of 5 Feb. under World Battle Fronts, "Closer to the Goal"? If not be sure to do so.

I don't know when I'll be able to get this in the mail but hope to before we get away from here. I received a letter from Mamma with her picture enclosed. I was amazed at how old it makes her look.

Have you ever had fertilizer (Vigoro) put around the pecan tree? It can use at least 5 pounds. Daddy can tell you how to spread it and dig it in. I have never received the P&L statement from Sylvan. If he hasn't sent it tell him to spend the extra 5¢ and send it air mail. Love to you and the Kiddies. I love you,

Billy

On February 13, 1945 Dad sent Mother the following (probably from Saipan or Tinian):

Gee Honey:

It sure is a pretty night. I just came down from the con where I had been sitting for over an hour – Nestled here in the shelter of the little harbor – under the very bright stars – it is hard to realize why anyone would want to fight a war. The stars are particularly bright – the Southern Cross to the South and Polaris to the North. You cannot see most of them in many latitudes. We were underway all last night and came in here this afternoon to anchor for the night. It is nice and smooth and a welcome relief from the rough anchorage which we last had. The trade winds blow fairly hard most of the time which cause the ocean to be rough but it is protected in here and as I have been up since 0400 I'll enjoy a smooth night's sleep. I don't sleep well when the ship rolls as it has been recently. Not too long ago the Japs held this island too and the results of our shelling and bombing when we took it, are very much in evidence.

Our mail service has been terrible and the last letter I wrote has not been taken from the ship yet so I don't know when this'll get off. Hope you and the children are well. Lots of love to you all.

I love you, Billy.

Lt. W. W. Doar, USNR

Resting in Saipan and Tinian and preparing for the invasion of Iwo Jima, Dad wrote this letter on February 14, 1945:

Dear Sugar:

hear news that a boat is coming for our mail this P.M. so I will write you one last letter in this envelope. Not that I'm sure it will get off by any means because we have been promised before but I hope.

We are taking it kind of easy today while at anchor and will probably get a swim this P.M. The weather is really delightful.

I've seen a lot these last few days and that is not all I'm going to see. Wish I could tell you about it and maybe the next time you receive mail from me I'll be able to write a little more freely. In the meantime keep your eyes and ears open.

Gee, I'd give anything to see you folks. I look at all of your pictures but that is not enough. I want to be with all of you and if I did not love all of you and home so much, I wouldn't even be here – it's worth fighting for.

Over and over again I love <u>all</u> of you. Billy

W. W. Doar
Lieut., USNR,
Commanding Officer

Dad wrote the following two letters edited by the censor (Dad was the Censor) on February 17 and 18, 1945:

Dear Sugar:

I was so busy yesterday that I did not get a chance to write and last night I was too tired. Last minute preparations, things that could not be done until now are taking a lot of our time. Other than that everything is routine. We had a submarine alert yesterday but it turned out to be negative. I think we would like to see a little action and before the sun goes down the third time I know that we will. The weather is fine and I hope it stays so.

Over the radio it says that carrier planes are continuing their attacks against the Tokyo area. They were scheduled of course to help out the (censored) operation. (Censored) is taking a terrific pounding from ships and planes. It is not much larger than Pawley's – no longer but wider. It is of volcanic origin and has caves like Saipan and Tinian – Guns are emplaced in those caves – There will be determined resistance. No matter what the headlines back home tell you the going will not be easy. We will take it of course because we'll overwhelm it but good American blood will stain the soil. It will be worth it because they will not then be able to raid B-29 bases on Saipan and Tinian and we will have a base within 700 miles to bomb Tokyo. The radio stated the above.

> *I think of you and my children always –*
> *and I love all of you.*
> *Billy*

Lieut. W. W. Doar USNR.

The battle for Iwo Jima began in earnest on February 19, 1945. Dad was concerned but not afraid. He wrote this letter on February 15, 1945 and added a post script on February 17, 1945:

Dear Sugar:

Mail came aboard as a pleasant surprise today just before we got underway. Most of the boys got letters. If the folks back home knew what mail means they would certainly write often. I received 6 letters from you including the one with the children's in it, and one from Mamma. I was certainly thankful. I really did not expect to receive any more mail because we had such a hard time getting a boat to take our mail ashore. It did finally get off yesterday tho. Of course this will not get into the mail until after we leave the target – (censored). Now I can tell you.

It is a small island less than 700 miles from Tokyo. It is well fortified and the Japs will probably make a determined effort to keep us from taking it. We have a vast force and will take it I am sure but even so it will be difficult as the Japs expect us. It has been bombed every day for the past 2 months and a half and shelled several times by our ships. Beginning tomorrow it will receive a terrific shellacking from ships and planes and unless the weather turns bad we go in on Monday the 19th. My ship is scheduled to go into the beach soon after the landings start.

I've often wondered how I'd fare in battle, so far I have been unable to "work up a scare". If I can just be as calm at the time as I have been thru the several rehearsals I'll be all right, and I'm sure that I will be.

We stopped in the Marshalls for a couple of days then came on to Saipan where we first anchored then moved just across the way to Tinian for a couple of days. They are quite pretty, tho nothing like Hawaii. In time the U.S. can probably devellop them into something worthwhile and these islands could be a new frontier. They would be much easier to devellop for instance than Alaska.

I'll try to write each night a little something until I can get them in the mail.

Tell the children I sure did appreciate and enjoy their letters. Bill said that he had been a good boy and I'm sure he had. I know by now that they have gotten over the mumps. Hope that Am had the other side too because she'll have it later if she didn't. I love them and miss them both so much. Gee what I'd give to see them – and I love you my darlin' – what I'd give to hold you close to me –

Love to you all,
Billy

W. W. Doar
Lieut., USNR,
Commanding Officer

Post Script on Feb. 17, 1945

Due to a change in censorship regulations, I had to delete the name of the target, but if you read the papers and listen to the radio you'll know as I have already heard more on the radio than I've written and this will not get into the mail until after we leave. B –

On February 17, 1945, Dad sent me the following letter. I was a month from 10 years old:

Dear Bill:

I just read your note again in which you tell me that you have the mumps. You also say that you have been good. I'm sure that you have been good, my sonny boy. Most of the time you are good and when you are not, you are not bad much. Keep on being good and when I get home we will have lots of good times hunting and fishing together.

I was thinking about you this morning and remembered when you were a tiny fellow that when I showed you something pretty you'd say "It is boopar" for it is beautiful and you'd say "my" for I. You are a big boy now and I'm proud of you, but I'll always remember what a sweet <u>little</u> boy you were. Be sweet to Julia and Amaryllis. They both love you and you must love them.

I'm glad that you are doing so well in school. Keep it up. I suppose you'll be playing baseball before long. I can remember when I liked for spring to come so I could play.

I love my sonny boy –
Daddy

W. W. Doar
Lieut., USNR,
Commanding Officer

The next day, February 18, 1945, he wrote my sister, Amaryllis, who is two years older than I:

Dear Amaryllis:

I sure was glad to get your nice little note. It is too bad that you had to have the mumps, but I "spect" that it is best go get over them. I did not get them until I was 16 and they are worse then. I'm sorry that you were prevented from being confirmed but that can be done later.

The weather has been hot and calm but today it has changed somewhat. While it is cooler it is also getting rougher. I hope that it doesn't get too rough because tomorrow will be a big day. I know you'll hear about it on the radio and read about it in the paper.

Our fleet has surely been knocking at the Japanese front door. The radio says they are shelling Iwo Jima, bombing the Bonins and Truk and made a 1500 plane raid around Tokyo. It takes a pretty big fleet to do all of that at one time.

I sure do miss my little girl – you are so sweet. I think of you so often and remember how you were my shadow when we lived at Kensington. We used to have great times together – and we will again when I get back.

I love my little sweetheart, Daddy

W. W. Doar
Lieut., USNR,
Commanding Officer

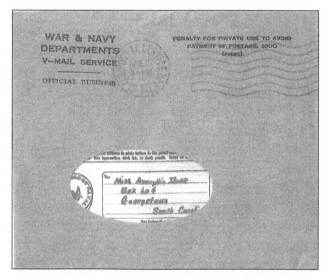

V-Mail was used in World War II.

As the fighting for Iwo Jima picked up, Dad remained concerned that he might not return home. He wrote the following letter expressing his concerns: *Feb. 18, 1945*

Dear Sugar:

I don't know why the censor regs. changed but maybe it is best not to disclose the identity of the location of the ship. However, the radio has already announced to the world what is going on so don't see why there should be objection to anyone writing about it. Anyway I'm in on an operation, I think that ought to pass –

I heard the Jap radio say this morning that they had sunk six of our battle ships, three carriers and destroyed 200 planes. Further, landings on the target had been repulsed with slaughter. At least the last is a joke because they have not started yet. By the time you receive this they will be complete.

I feel very confident of our part. Of course, a great deal depends on individual luck. While the operation will be successful no man can say who will and who will not come out alive. I think I will but if I don't that is the way I was meant to go – and maybe it is better to die for a cause than just to lay down and die.

From a business standpoint I feel good about the fact that you and the children will have a reasonable amount of insurance to see you thru. Put it on an income basis as I suggested and <u>don't</u> invest it or loan any of it to <u>anyone</u>. It is for you and them so leave what you don't need immediately on an income basis with the Insurance Co. that is the surest way to keep it. Of course there will be some kind of payment and pension from the government in addition.

I'm just writing the above so you'll know, "in case". If anything happens you'll know it <u>before</u> you receive this letter so don't worry when you do receive it.

Don't do any extra "moanin'". I know that you love me and that it will hurt you if I die but life has to go on and we have two fine children to bring up. It would not be right to influence their personalities by undue sadness.

I know that I have not always been what a good husband should be. I've done things that I'd give plenty to erase. Regardless of what I did I have loved you for the past twenty years and you've made me a good and understanding wife for the past 15 years. If after a time you feel that you have found someone else that will be kind to you and the children, don't deny him the happiness you could give him but go on and marry him. I have faith in your judgement.

Please don't think that I feel that I am a doomed man – to the contrary I do not but no one can tell what tomorrow's rising sun will bring forth nor what changes will occur by its setting. I just have a few minutes to set my thoughts down on paper and I'm telling you what I would if I were there. The best laid plans of man and mice sometimes go awry.

That's about all my sweet, if I die I want you to know that I think of and love you and the children. I'm sure that you do know it. If I live which I am reasonably sure that I will I'll be there by 1 July 1946 to tell you about it.

All my love to you and the children.

Billy –

P.S. The Tokyo radio started blaring forth again but apparently ran out of something to say as it just as suddenly stopped.

W. W. Doar
Lieut., USNR,
Commanding Officer

On February 21, 1945, the battle for Iwo Jima was raging. Dad was not scared.

Dear Sugar:

We are in the third day of the battle now. I heard via radio that operations were proceeding satisfactorily. That is true and makes good headlines but those that do not know are apt to dismiss it too lightly. It has been tough, too tough. The weather was good the first day but yesterday the wind blew up cold and it started raining and today is cold, rough and cloudy.

The damned Japs are licked but don't seem to know it. In spite of incessant shelling by ships, day and night and constant air strikes by our planes the bastards are still fighting hard. (Several hours later) – I'll try to pick up where I left off. The first day we went right in close after the initial landings and thru the glasses could see pretty well what was going on. Progress was pretty slow. We were expecting to be called in any time to beach but we were not. Some of our sister ships carrying tanks were and they drew fire.

Yesterday morning we were laying off-shore about 5000 yards and the Japs began firing at us with 40 MM shells. They were hitting all around us and bursting. You should have seen us get out further. One piece of shrapnel came aboard and hit a man but did not puncture his life jacket. He is keeping it for a souvenir. After that whenever we got in close we drew that fire.

Finally just before noon our call came to go into the beach. I had wondered if I'd be scared. It may sound like a lie but I wasn't a bit. We had a place on the beach to land between a wrecked small boat and a wrecked tank. It was just about 20 feet wider than the ship. Just before we hit the beach a shell hit inshore from us – about 200 yards. We were on the beach 32 minutes and several shells hit within 250 yards. One burst overhead from our stern and shrapnel hit the deck, luckily hitting no one. We made a perfect beaching.

From the water's edge in front of us on up the hill on each side and in front were thousands of our men – some of them dead. Tanks had gotten up the hill to the Jap airfield but not many men had been able to follow them because the fire was too intense. Of course there are many other things I'd like to tell you about it but for several reasons including time and space cannot.

This morning about 0800 a pretty big shell came out our way but passed overhead sounding like a RR train.

As I write this we have just received orders to standby to go into the beach again to discharge our cargo. The enemy is still shooting at the beach and I sure do hope

*that they do not get our range. I'm not scared but really
I don't want to die – I'd like to take two drinks and sleep
for a week tho – It has been kind of strenuous. Well
here's love to all of you. I'll add to this later.*

Love, Billy
Lt. W. W. Doar, USNR

On February 22, 1945 Dad describes landing on
the beach at Iwo Jima (Mr. Wyche was the Executive
Officer of LSM-60):

Well Sugar:

*We went in! After standing by for hours we could
see that the Japs were shelling the beach where we were
supposed to go. Then they hit one of our ammunition
dumps right where we were supposed to go and it started
exploding all over the place. They held us out until it
burned out. In the meantime, our ships and planes went
to work on the Jap guns. Finally about 1730 we got
the word to go in and we did. Apparently our side had
gotten in some good work because we were on the beach
about 50 minutes and nothing came our way. Mr. Wyche
said that the Marines on the beach told him that the
Japs were scheduled to start shelling the beach again
at 1845. I don't know how they knew but we took their
word for it and unloaded as fast as we could and did not
tarry when we finished. (Many hours later) I do not
know whether they started exactly on schedule but they
did shell the beach after we left.*
*War is not a very pretty sight. Dead men were lying
around. Some of them were partially burned. There
is a terrible expenditure of equipment. The beach was
so littered that we had a hard time getting on it. In
spite of the hardships at Valley Forge, etc. I believe that*

Farther George would be appalled today – and the rain which has been falling for two day is just as cold and disagreeable today as it was then. I haven't had my clothes off since I put them on four days ago and none of us have had more than 4 hours sleep a night. Of course the boys on the beach don't get that much and they are right out in the rain all of the time.

We are now loading a high priority cargo of inflammables and ammunition so we'll probably beach again this P.M. Haven't been in close today so do not know whether the beach will be "hot" or not. Believe that our luck will hold tho and we'll come out O.K.

Kiss my babies for me. I'll add to this later.
I love you. Billy.

The Beach head at Iwo Jima.

Feb. 23, 1945

Sugar: The going has been tough and we will work all night. Progress was good today tho and about three more days should wind it up. The Japs have gotten in some punches tho. You remember Capt. Pratt and Lt. Thayer. I hope they were among the survivors. I'm too tired to think much less write.

Good night. I love you Billy.

W. W. Doar
Lieut., USNR,
Commanding Officer

Dad received mail from Dr. F. A. Bell, our family physician, Judge Higgins, the local Magistrate, Senator (Dr.) Olin Sawyer and our dentist, Dr. E. W. Durant. Dr. Durant wrote Dad the following on February 23, 1945:

Dear Walter:

Well, after a long time I have finally decided to surprise you with a letter. First I want to thank you for thinking of me. I should have answered your card on V-mail long before this, but better late than never. Just talked to Miss Julia not over five minutes ago. Said she was feeling fine. Saw Amarilla (sp) and Bill yesterday afternoon while on my way to supper. They are sweet children – so polite, which means so much, especially to older folks.

Old Georgetown is just the same. Know your sweet lady keeps you posted with all the local news. I try to keep as busy as possible for work is really the only "honest to God" contentment.

I think of you often and wish for you all the good luck

in the world. Take good care of No. 1 and hurry back.

Your old friend, E. W. Durant

Although the battle raged on, Dad continued to write. The following is his letter to my mother dated March 1, 1945:

Dear Sugar:

I got a letter off on a ship leaving this area last night so I hope that you get it in about 10 days. We are alongside a ship now that has a post office so I'll mail this in hopes that it gets off soon.   I'm   still well and well-fed. We were able to get some more ice cream yesterday and will have it today. Gee, I'm tired and sleepy tho. I had one good night's sleep but I was just as sleepy the next morning as when I went to bed. Since then sleep has never been more than 4 hours in 24.

The battle still goes on. I have a ringside seat right now. The yellow bastards just will not give up. They are shelled, bombed, strafed and fired on by everything we have but they have to be rooted out one by one. They kill themselves at the last minute rather than be captured. They are surely fanatically bold and brave.

Radio Tokyo makes extravagant claims that could not possibly be so but it is tough enough at that. Don't let anyone say or think that the war is over. Here in the Pacific it is just <u>beginning</u>. It will be 1 July before it ends in Germany. I love you and the babies. Give my love to Mamma and Daddy.

Billy
We still have received no mail but hope to today.
Lt. W. W. Doar USNR

On March 2, 1945 Dad wrote Mother a V-mail:

Dear Sugar:

There is not much to write about. It seems to go on forever. Sleep is hard to get and we are all pretty tired but there is a job to be done so we carry on. I know that this grind will not last always and we will have a chance to rest some day.

I've put several letters on ships that were moving out of this area so I suppose that you will get them eventually. Don't know when this will leave the ship. We have had no mail in two weeks. It sure would help all of us if we could get some. It will arrive eventually of course. Each day we hope.

The weather is rough today and a cold wind blows most of the time. After the sun goes down it is biting. I was in it most of last night. We do have plenty of good hot food tho and that is more than the boys on the beach do because they are mostly eating out of cans. There'll be better times tho. Give my love to the babies. I think of and love all of you.

Billy

The battle for Iwo Jima is going well as reported by

Dad on March 4, 1945 and March 5, 1945:

Dear Sugar:

I haven't written in a couple of days because: 1. I've been too busy, 2. There has been little to write about, and 3. We still have to depend on other ships to get our mail out.

The fight still goes on but the resistance is gradually weakening and three or four more days should see the end of organized resistance. There will still be some left to root out of caves tho. They are a bold and ruthless enemy but fanatically brave and apparently do not mind dying.

Day before yesterday while we were on the beach they began shelling all around us. One hit less than 100 yards away and shrapnel hit our sides. We could see our poor fellows on the beach cut down as the shells hit. That went on for about 30 minutes before our planes located the battery and knocked it out. It certainly made me feel easier when it stopped. None of my crew has been hit yet and I sure don't want them to be. Yesterday and today they could not shell the beach. Hope they never can again.

Our organization and the equipment we have landed is amazing. I expect a city to blossom out any day now. The radio says our fleet bombed and shelled one of their islands within 350 miles of Tokyo last night. Hope they catch hell –

Love to you and the babies –Billy

Lt. W. W. Doar USNR

Then on March 5, 1945 he wrote:

Dear Sugar:

The same grind. We are at it 24 hours a day. I was able to get a little sleep this morning tho so I feel somewhat refreshed this afternoon.

The Japs still haven't quit altho they are now hopelessly outnumbered and backed up into one corner of the island. They are not using their banzai tactics here like they did in many places. That makes it necessary to hunt out each one and kill him in order to eliminate him.

I've seen many brave men here but I believe the

bravest was a plane pilot. The Japs hit the plane and set it on fire. The plane was headed out toward our ships and losing altitude rapidly. Instead of jumping, the pilot stuck with it until he got it headed away from the ships – and then too late jumped. He was so close to the water that his parachute did not open – He kept the plane away from our ships but lost his life. Brave man!

In our present cargo there was a lot of candy. One of the cases broke open so we now have enough candy to last us for weeks. Wish I could send the kids some of the Hershey bars. Hope they have now entirely recovered from the mumps. I'm sure they have. We have not yet received any mail which is bad. Suppose it will come in a lump. Lots of love to all.

Billy

Lt. W. W. Doar USNR. -

Much later –

I wish I could be there to help you plant the garden and raise some chickens. I love to see things grow. It would be so much better to do constructive things rather than see so much destruction. I'm afraid it will be a long long time before I can do that tho.

I have never received the P&L statement of the store. I'd like to see it. Please get it from Sylvan and send it to me.

It will be fine if you can get to spend 3 weeks on the beach. It will do the children a lot of good and I know that they will enjoy it. Get Bill's fishing line rigged so that he can fish. When I was his age I was quite a fisherman and enjoyed it so much. He will too if he ever starts catching fish. It is hard to realize that he will be 10 years old tomorrow.

I've never received the prayer books which Mr. Bull sent but suppose I will in time. We have had no time for *services recently as <u>working</u>, eating and a <u>little</u> sleeping is about all we can do.*

 It will probably be Easter by the time you receive this. Flowers will be in bloom. I'd love to see them – and I'd love to see you and the children.

Billy

Lt. W. W. Doar USNR

On March 8, 1945 Dad wrote Mother. He was delighted to receive mail from family and friends:

Dear Sugar:

Mail was a very welcome visitor aboard yesterday as it was the first we have had since Feb. 15. I had 11 letters from you, 3 from Mamma, 1 from Bachman, he said nothing, 1 from Arthur Joseph and one from Aunt Min. Your nice valentine was included. There were 3 letters missing from you so I suppose I'll get them next time. The watch has not come yet but suppose it will in due time. Regular mail takes more than 30 days to reach me.

There is nothing new. We are still worked to death and regular sleep is hard to get. The battle still goes on. We are slowly winning but the Japs can take a terrible lot of punishment. They are holed up in caves with connecting tunnels. When our men smoke them out of one cave they go on to the next and we have to do the same thing all over again. I just witnessed an air strike by our planes. It was wonderfully coordinated and beautifully executed, but I'm afraid did not accomplish the desired results. After all they cannot fly into the caves.

The weather is rough and raw today. Almost like a

day in November at home. However, the temperature is about 60.

I'm very <u>glad</u> that the children have recovered from the mumps. Their reports are fine and I'm proud of them. I've just received a call so I'll have to finish this later.

Mar. 9, 1945

Dear Julie:

Last night only 2 hours sleep and gee there was a cold wind. Today has been raw again. I was able to get a few hours disturbed sleep this A.M. Tonight we should be able to sleep until about 4 A.M.

I'm enclosing some more Jap money. There are several different kinds. If Bill is keeping it in his album he should have one of each kind and the duplicates go to you and Am. Sorry I do not have duplicates all around. I washed it with plenty of soap but as it came off of a dead Jap. Tell them <u>not</u> to put it in their mouths. There are also two coins.

Looks like we are going to stay around here for a while and unload the ships which come in. That will get awful monotonous after a while. I'd like to move on to something else.

The fighting still goes on – Those caves are surely tough nuts to crack. The devils are licked but will not quit. The trouble is it takes American lives to root them out.

Haven't been able to get much news on the radio for two days. Hope the war in Europe will not last beyond April but it will probably be 1 July. When we get all of our men out here maybe we can wind it up in a couple of years. I love you and the children.

Billy

W. W. Doar
Lieut., USNR,
Commanding Officer

On March 11, 1945, Dad wrote to Mother:

Dear Sugar!

I sent the "mailman" for the mail today and he brought <u>one</u> piece of mail for the entire ship. It <u>was</u> my watch. It arrived safely and seems to be keeping good time. Thanks a thousand times for having it fixed and sending it to me. I'm sure the watch never had any idea of travelling so far – and I only wish that I could have <u>brought</u> it home if only to stay as long (or short) as it did. Again, thank you.

I think you did right in deciding that we should not move the store. Besides I am under the impression that we leased the building now occupied for 3 years.

Progress is still slow here but it seems to be sure. Our work has slacked off a little and we had a fairly good sleep last night for a change. Don't know how it will be tonight tho. The weather is still raw and to us cold, altho the temperature is actually above 55.

There is nothing else to write about. Mail is pretty slow in coming thru. It would help if it got to us faster but I suppose they do the best they can. I also suppose that it is pretty slow in leaving here, but we do get it away from the ship a little faster than we did.

Don't know what will be in store for us when we leave here. Hope they give us a chance to go somewhere and rest but as we are definitely on the offensive they might send us on to the next target wherever and whenever that may be.

Give my love to the babies – Also to Mama and daddy. I write them whenever I can.

Lots of love, Billy

W. W. Doar
Lieut., USNR,
Commanding Officer

On March 13, 1945, Daddy wrote to my Mother:

Dear Sugar!

The excitement of urgency is gone and the grind has become monotonous. The last few days we have come in contact with the Merchant Marine. They and their unions work by the clock and they are generally louses. It is a crying shame the way they do right here in the face of the enemy. I had heard stories of them before – some of which were in print and later denied, but I'm experiencing it now and believe me if I ever get the chance I'm going to put in my two cents worth about it.

I suppose you will receive this letter just after your birthday – your 41st anniversary. Many happy returns. Again I'm going to tell you to buy something for yourself and leave it to you as to what it is. You have the checkbook so use it.

The weather is still disagreeably cool. We have been used to <u>hot</u> weather so long that we feel it more I suppose.

War news is good for our side. They seem to be "going to town" in Germany again. Hope they can roll that up in a short time – but the Germans may still have

*another offensive left. Japan is beginning to feel our
bombers. The radio said that our planes are using the
newly captured airfield on Iwo Jima to blast the Japs
on nearby islands. The Japanese homeland is just now
beginning to feel the pinch of war but I am afraid it will
only make them fight harder. They are fanatical in their
fighting now. That B-29 raid on Tokyo is a sample of
what Germany has been getting. Planes help a lot but
they cannot do the job alone. The <u>infantryman</u> has to go
in and root the enemy out. I've seen that demonstrated
right here.*

*Give my love to the babies.
I miss all of you so much – Lots of love to all,*

Billy

Lt. W. W. Doar, USNR
*P.S. The watch is keeping good time.
Thanks a million –*

My Dad wrote the following to my Mother on March
14, 1945:

Dear Julie:

*I hope to get the mail off the ship a little later so I'll
write this last note to you. Your letters to me are not
censored so you can say what you like.*

*You say you envy Lucy going to New York to see C.
G. – but if I were there you wouldn't come so it is no use
to envy – As a matter of fact you could have come to
San Diego and wouldn't. But don't worry. I will not be
anywhere near that close for a good many months.*

*There is really not very much to write about that
I have not already written about. The Marines seem
to have the situation pretty well in hand now – altho
fighting is still going on. It seems that they just have to
wear down the remnants of the Jap garrison which they*

are doing. Time of 26 Feb. and 5 March gives a fair account but by no means tell all.

The weather is a little more pleasant today and I hope it stays that way. I do not enjoy being cold. I got a full night's sleep last night and that makes me feel better. We are short on water tho so I cannot take a bath. Seems like we just can't have everything. The poor devils on the beach haven't had a bath in a moth – and are still eating out of cans and sleep – when they can – on the ground.

Hope your Red Cross drive was successful. Be sure to give at least $5.00 from the store.

> *Lots of love to you all, Billy*

W. W. Doar
Lieut., USNR,
Commanding Officer

Tell Dr. DuRant I appreciated his
Letter. Will keep on the lookout for Ned.

Dad wrote the following letter to my Mother dated March 14, 1945:

Sweetie:

Mail came aboard quite unexpectedly yesterday afternoon. Ten letters from you! Thru March 2, two from Mamma – a note from Dr. DuRant and one from Blaha who used to be in my crew at Ft. Lauderdale.

Of course I knew that I'on Weston had been wounded at Saipan. It was my (shall I say not so) subtle way of telling you I was on the way there. Next time I'll try to draw a picture.

I'm sorry you were sick but as that was almost a month ago suppose that you are entirely recovered by now.

I enjoyed Bill's letter and am so glad he liked the post

card. I have been trying to get him a Jap stamp. I've seen only one and could not get that one.

You'd better let that baby stuff ride until I get there. Then if you still have it in mind I'll see what I can do about fixing you up.

Resistance here is slowly lessening. I understand that they have the Japs cornered in two pockets and are slowly closing in. The Commanding General is in one and they were to take them alive but, like the others, will surely kill himself at the last moment.

By all means go to Pawley's with the children in June. It will cost something extra but will be worth it. We can afford it.

Lots of love to you all, Billy

W. W. Doar
Lieut., USNR
Commanding Officer

My Daddy wrote me this short letter on March 14, 1945:

Dear Bill:

I was able to get you some Jap letters and post cards for your album today. Don't put them in your mouth. They were taken from dead men.

There are a couple of duplicates which you might give to Amaryllis.

I received and enjoyed your letters. Keep writing to me.

Hope you have a big time at the beach in June. Get your fishing line out and catch some fish for me.

Your report was fine. Keep it up. Give my love to Amaryllis.

Daddy loves you.

Lt. W. W. Doar USNR

(Attached to this letter was the following article which my Daddy apparently cut from a military magazine:)

Marines Reach Summit Of Mt.Suribachi On

The war was brought closer to Tokyo this week, when American Marines invaded the Japanese island of Iwo Jima, only 700 miles from the Nippon capital.

Sunday evening, it was announced that the initial invasion of this important island had commenced. The Yanks pushed forward in the face of fanatical resistance and during the first three days of the invasion were ahead of schedule. On Tuesday, they seized an important landing field and future conquests appeared imminent. However, even fiercer Japanese resistance and counterattacks slowed the Yanks to a standstill after they had established a 2½ mile beachhead.

On Thursday, Admiral Nimitz revealed that another division of marines had been put ashore and this swelled the total of men in the landing force to over 45,000. An estimated 800 ships were used in the operation. At this time also, Nimitz announced that cas-

ualties were officially placed as in excess of 3,600, proof that this battle is even bloodier than Tarawa.

Early on Friday, Adm. Nimitz announced that U. S. task units involved in the landing operation had sustained some damage from attacking Nipponese fighters and bombers. The death toll was lifted to 4,553 officially. Rain and rough seas offered another hazard to the bringing in of supplies and reinforcements. If it were not for the fact that such a huge advance had been made in the beginning, the invasion might have been doomed for an ignominious and costly defeat.

Some of the obstacles that the Marines are forced to overcome are heavily sown land mines, deep volcanic sands which impede the moving of heavy equipment, such as mobile guns, tanks, and tank destroyers, and the suicidal stand of the Japanese troops

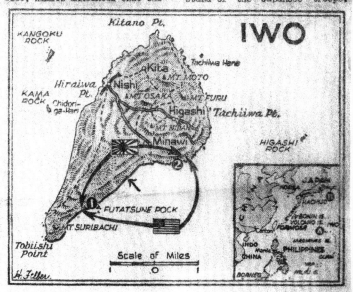

49

On March 16, 1945, my Daddy wrote to my Mother:

Dear Julie:

This letter will contain several trinkets. There are some Jap stamps for Bill – duplicates for Amaryllis if she wants them. There are also three slivers from a _real_ Jap Zero. They were cut from the rising sun insignia, but this sun will be set forever. Each of you can have a sliver.

The Admiral officially secured the island two days ago but apparently the Japs didn't hear about it yet because they keep on fighting. It is in the nature of "mopping up" tho and organized resistance is just about at an end.

Please don't let the children put any of this stuff in their mouth. It may be well to spread it all out in a box and put it out in the sun for several hours.

The weather has been delightful for the past two days and we have resumed sunbathing. We are beginning to get back to normal now and sleep comes a little more regularly. I'm glad too because we are pretty tired.

I've let my mustache grow out again. It is too much a part of me to do away with. I'll continue to wear my hair "crew" stile because it is more comfortable that way and I'm afraid that the tooth will not grow back.

I understand that we have some mail at the post office ship but we haven't been able to go get it. Maybe we can in a day or two.

> *Lots of love to all of you.   Billy*
Lt. W. W. Doar, USNR
Commanding Officer

On March 17, 1945, Daddy wrote to Mother:

Dear Julie:

We have been so busy that we still haven't had time to go by the P.O. ship and get our mail. Maybe we will be able to do so this afternoon.

The weather has turned much cooler and is "blowing up" which makes it uncomfortable. Wish it would stay warm like it was for the past two days.

It was announced that organized resistance has ended but all of the Japs didn't get the word yet so mopping up continues.

There wasn't much sleep again last night so we are all pretty tired today. Two more days and we will have been here a month. How the months are passing. Days, weeks and months out of our lives away from our loved ones that can never be replaced. I censor a good many letters. However, it may be expressed, the theme of all of them is the same – "How I miss you and wish that the war would end so that I could come back to you." We have a few aboard that are really babies. Believe it or not they are among our best men. They have not had enough "experience" to want to do it some other way and do as they are told. Most of the little trouble that we have comes from some wise guy that wants to do it his way. We have one very good man aboard who used to be on a DE. He has gotten fouled up several times because he wants to tell us how they did so and so on the DE – but happens not to be practicable aboard an LSM.

Take good care of my babies.

I miss and love all of you - Billy

Don't subscribe to the Times for me again. Newspapers just don't get out this far.

I subscribed to the airmail edition of Time and get that fairly regular. Magazines are few and far between.

Lt. W. W. Doar, USNR

On March 19, 1945, my Daddy wrote to my Mother:

Dear Sugar!

I received your letters of 28 Feb. and 3 and 5 March on Friday on Friday. Yesterday mail came aboard too but there was not a single letter for me. Suppose I'll get several the next time we get mail.

I am enclosing a letter I received from Thayer on Friday. I'm glad to know they are allright. They must have had <u>some</u> experience. Hope I never have to duplicate it.

Things are getting back to normal again. Last night we were able to lay at anchor and a full night's sleep was very welcome.

Yesterday and today the weather has been rough and cold. Hope it turns off better as it is unpleasant. We do have heat but it is <u>always</u> necessary for several to be topside and "take" it.

I'm sure that the children came out all right on their exams. They are smart and if they get their work from day to day there is no need to fear exams.

By the time you get this it will be April! One of the best months at home. I understand that April and May are rather rough and stormy in this area. Hope it is not too disagreeable. Looks like we <u>might</u> be here during that time. The Navy changes my mind pretty often tho so there's no telling.

Time of Feb 25, March 5 & 12 tells part of the story. You would have to <u>be here</u> to get it all. "Brave, brave men", those Marines!

Hope all of you are well. I am and as well satisfied as possible away from my loved ones.

Give my love to all – Lots of love

Billy

Lt. W. W. Doar USNR

In Dad's letter of March 20, 1945, to Mother.

Dear Sugar!

Two nights to sleep in a row! I am just not used to it and so last night couldn't sleep. Couldn't get to sleep the first part of the night and woke up at 0400. Looks like I'll take some adjusting to get back to normal.

Suppose I'll take some adjusting to get back to normal when I get home too. I've been telling people what to do for so long and expecting them to do it that I don't know how I am going to react when you start telling me what to do again.

The weather is still windy, rough and raw. Wish this part of the country could make up its mind whether it is winter or spring. The hills on the island are beginning to turn green. The grass is beginning to come out after the terrible "plowing" the shells gave it. Practically all of the trees and shrubbery were laid flat.

The news by radio continues good for our side. You just don't see why the Germans keep on or how they do. But then it was very difficult to understand how the Japs could keep on here. At the end of the 4th day the Tokyo radio said that the Jap general had made the statement that he was determined to die here. Apparently he did because I've never heard that he was captured. Apparently the Japs buried him. Practically the entire 20,000 odd of them were killed. The last I heard only about 100 prisoners had been taken and resistance was narrowed down to about 200 in a block house which it took several days for us to take. All organized resistance has now ceased but there are still some individuals to be rooted out – and probably will be in the caves for several months yet.

There was no mail yesterday and not much prospect of any today. Hope you and the babies are well.

Lots of love to all of you
Billy

Lt. W. W. Doar, USNR

And on March 22, 1945 Dad writes:

Dear Sugar:

There is not much to say but I'll add a little bit to what I said yesterday. There was not much sleep last night but I was able to get in a couple of hours this morning. It helped some but I am still pretty tired.

The wind is very strong today which makes it rough. Wish it would clear up. –

Hours later. The C.O. of the ship we are tied up to asked me to lunch with him so I did. He has been out here for 3 years and has <u>seen</u> some things.

I just learned we can get mail away from the ship <u>immediately</u>.

There's really nothing else to write about anyway.

Love to you and my babies, Billy

Lt. W. W. Doar, USNR.

On March 23, 1945, Dad wrote to Mother:

Dear Sugar:

Today was pay day but I didn't draw any money. I haven't drawn any since I first got to Pearl in December and now I have $519.00 on the books. What a party I'm going to have if I ever get to a place where I can have one! I had $30.00 in my wallet when I left Hawaii and I still have it. My mess bill comes out automatically and *is only $21.00 a month. Many of the crew drew money, why I don't know because there is nothing to spend it for. A Marine came aboard the other day with a Jap flag that he wanted to sell for $50.00. I would like to have had it but I still haven't lost the sense of the value of money that much.*

The weather is somewhat more pleasant today because it is warmer than it has been but a strong wind is still blowing. Wish it would stop but I understand that it blows here most of the time.

Most of my chocolate bars are gone. I had 50 1-ounce bars. I thought about sending the whole package home but it would have cost $6.00 by air mail and regular mail would take 2 months and they'd probably spoil. So I've eaten most of them myself. Anyway I thought about you and the children while eating them and wished that you could have some. We get plenty of stuff like that and plenty of cigarettes. I haven't bought any in a couple of months.

It has been almost a week since we've had any mail but we have been able to send outgoing mail away from the ship. Hope that it gets on its way and that you are receiving it.

I've never received the Prayer books which Mr. Bull sent to me. Suppose they will arrive some day and we'll be glad to get them when they come.

We are not quite as busy as we were but still have plenty to do. The radio says we are lambasting Japan again which makes me feel good. The harder the better – They will have to be torn limb from limb before they quit.

Hope you and the babies are well.
Lots of love to you all. Billy

Lt. W. W. Doar, USNR

In a letter dated May 8, 1945, Dad defends man's best friend, Wag, his Labrador Retriever. It is beyond me why my Mother apparently referred to Wag as a sin.

Dear Sugar:

Your letters of 25 and 26 April, enclosing one from Am, and one from Mama and Lucas came this P.M. They sure do help.

I am distressed about "Sonny" Siau. It hurts even more when it happens to someone you know. But as you say, it could have been worse. It was <u>worse</u> for at least 4000 at Iwo Jima. I remember talking to one wounded man who (among others) was evacuated from the beachhead on this ship. His leg was badly shot up and I was commiserating with him. His reply was that anyone who left that island alive should be thankful. Even minus a leg Sonny is alive and pretty apt to stay that way for he is now out of the war.

We have heard the unofficial announcement of the capitulation of Germany. The official announcement is to be made at 1300 Greenwich time. That is 2300 here and 0900 there. We probably will not get it until tomorrow morning.

I was talking to two Army fliers last night and they are quite optimistic (wish I could be) about the early end of the war with Japan. They say that our fliers in fighter planes regularly fly right down the main streets of Kobe, Yokohama and Tokyo with machine guns blazing and meet only feeble resistance from Jap Ack Ack or planes. They are laying bets that the war will be over before the end of this summer. I hope so but do not see how it can be in spite of the fact that the Jap air force has been decisively defeated and their Navy reduced to *impotence. It takes <u>time</u> to route them out of their holes. They still <u>think</u> they are winning the war because their leaders say so. All they have to do is put up with a little hard work and inconveniences and they will inherit the earth, they ae told. They will continue to fight.*

"Wag" is good. Why couldn't you substitute "Jet" for "Sin". She is not sinful. She is one of the best friends I have. I do not think that I would try to keep her shut in. She is getting old and if a car happens to kill her, that is the way she was meant to go. Better get some flea powder and dust her and rub it into her coat once or twice a week. Dipping would be better but I know you'd never get her in that barrel. She will enjoy the beach.

Am says she wants to go to Columbia while you are on the beach. You know I don't want to be arbitrary about it but I sure do believe that she will have a better time at Pawley's and I <u>know</u> it will do her more good. Columbia is terribly hot in June and crowded besides. Everyone who is in Columbia wants to come to the beach. Am can swim and fish and catch crabs. I think that would be much more fun than running around hot, crowded Columbia standing in line to get in the stuffy picture shows. Where is she going to camp?

I am enclosing a 15¢ air mail stamp for Bill. Don't know whether he wants it or not. He can throw it away if he doesn't. He should have received the foreign currency I sent him by now and <u>know</u> that he will like that. Tell the little cuss to write me sometime.

I enjoyed Am's nice letter. She writes well and her penmanship is improving. Keep up the good work!

I have been up quite late both last night and the night before so I am tired tonight. We are at anchor and sure do hope I will not be called in the middle of the night to go alongside a cargo ship to start loading. If they will wait until 0800 it will suit me fine.

> *Hope all of you continue fine.*
> *Lots of love to all. I love you, <u>Billy</u>*

The price of that wood is outrageous. Daddy should know <u>someone</u> who has it cheaper than that. Coal must certainly be cheaper in comparison.

W. W. Doar,
Lieut., USNR,
Commanding Officer

On June 13, 1945, Dad wrote to my Mother. He was on his way back home:

Dear Sugar:

There is really nothing to write about and I have been out of touch with you so long that it is hard to make up anything. We are bucking these seas kicked up by the trade winds and it is so rough that is pretty uncomfortable. In fact, the ship pitches and rolls so much that it is hard to write. We are in the low latitudes and but for the wind it would be pretty hot. Having to keep everything closed down makes it stuffy. There is one consolation – we are headed for semi-civilization.

Ever since last night we have been passing near Jap held islands. Evidently the Navy feels that it is safe for they routed us this way. I'll feel better about it when we finally get thru them tomorrow sometime because those bastards play for keeps and they play rough. I sure do hope that all of you are on the island. I know it will be nice there. When we reach destination 17 about 10 days from now our mail should be there and I'll enjoy bringing myself up to date with your letters.

Hope all are well. I'll add to this from time to time.

I love all of you,
Billy

Lt. W. W. Doar, USNR

On June 17, 1945, my Dad wrote this to my Mother:

Dear Sugar:

Here I am at six o'clock in the morning writing a letter. The sun rose at 0500 this morning which meant we had to be at GQ at 0430. If it had not have been so early it would have been a beautiful sunrise but I am beginning to agree with Yates Snowden that the sunrise is a horrible sight.

We spent two days as Sat. 16 June – one on each side of the International Date Line. Now we are back at the same day and date as you are. At least that is a little reassuring.

Last night the moon and stars were very beautiful, the only drawback being we were in mid Pacific and at least 1000 miles to the nearest land of any kind. The wind and sea have become more moderate and we are able to make much better time and are more comfortable. Hope it stays this way or even improve a little.

That is about all I know except that I miss all of you terribly and yearn for the day that we can all be back together again.

I expect to be able to get this mailed by the end of the week and trust there will be many letters from you waiting for me.

Lots of love to all, Billy

W. W. Doar
Lieut., USNR,
Commanding Officer

59

On June 20, 1945, my Dad wrote to my Mother:

Dear Sugar:

Well in spite of everything we have made pretty good time and unless something goes wrong we should be safely in our destination port tomorrow night. I'll truly be glad. We have been on the way for more than three weeks. It has been rough and tiresome and sleep has been hard to get.

I do not know whether I'll get to see Lucas or not but I sure am going to try to. Anyway, I'll be able to go to the "O" club and take a few drinks – And go to town and at least <u>see</u> a woman pass by (it's almost been six months) and best of I'll be able to lie down and sleep the night thru without being called or without the ship rolling so much that I cannot sleep. Also I should have plenty of mail and I'll read to my heart's content.

I sure do hope that you and the children are all fine.

I miss and love you, Billy

W. W. Doar
Lieut., USNR,
Commanding Officer

On June 21, 1945, my Dad wrote:

Dear Sugar:

Well it seems like luck was "agin" us. We were going along nicely and would have reached our destination by noon today but about 0315 one of the ships developed trouble so here we are limping along at about 5 knots and so will not reach port until tomorrow a.m. I had counted on a good night's sleep tonight and boy could I use it – but no such luck. We will be underway again tonight. Well it could have happened a thousand or so miles back and that would have meant a terrible delay –

so it is that much to be thankful for.

The weather this a.m. is not so rough. In fact it is pretty nice. That's good too.

Nothing much else to say. This should get into the mail tomorrow afternoon but it may be the next day. I'm feeling good but I sure am tired and need rest. Hope that you and the children are well.

Lots of love to all of you. Billy

And on July 8, 1945 a Western Union telegram sent from San Francisco, California, addressed to:

Mrs. W. W. Doar

107 Cannon St.

was received by my Mother on July 9, 1945 and had the following message:

"OKAY BABY STAND BY IT WONT BE LONG NOW LOVE   ALL ."

BILLY."

Dad was at Camp Perry, Williamsburg, Virginia, the Navy Distribution Center, and wrote this letter on September 10, 1945:

Dear Sugar:

It sure was nice to talk to you on Saturday and I hope that before many days I'll be able to talk to you morning, noon and night. You see, I love you.

It was a nice diversion to spend the weekend with Bachman and Liz and they were lovely to me. They had Joe and a couple to go down to the Pine Tree Inn and we had a steak supper Saturday night. It was good steak. We all had a good time and Joe and I particularly enjoyed telling sea stories. Bachman and Liz brought me back last night arriving here about 2100.

This morning your two sweet letters were here and this afternoon the orders you sent arrived. I'll start the ball to rolling for claiming your travel tomorrow.

Under the new 1/4 point for overseas duty which will become effective on Friday the 15th, I will be eligible for release from active duty six days earlier than the 21st. It takes about two weeks to get thru the mill tho – so I suppose it will still be 1 October before I get there.

This is the hottest day I have spent since this time last year at Houston and Galveston. I'm glad I don't have anything to do.

Well Sugar that's about all I know. I'll be there just as soon as the Navy will let me.

Tell my babies
I love them and I do love you.
<u>Billy</u>

Bachman Doar was Dad's first cousin but raised by my Grandmother Lizzie as Dad's brother. Liz was Bachman's wife. Joe was Commander Joseph L. Bull, a boyhood friend, stationed near Norfolk, Virginia. Camp Perry is now or in the past was a CIA Training Center.

Dad came home from the war exuding patriotism. He promptly joined the American Legion, the V.F.W. and the 40 and 8 veterans' organizations. He became Commander of American Legion Post 114 in July, 1946, and he was very active in the V.F.W. He became Chef de Gare of the Georgetown 40 and 8. He often made patriotic speeches to these organizations on Veterans' Days.

"Solger" Doar at dedication of Marion Park.

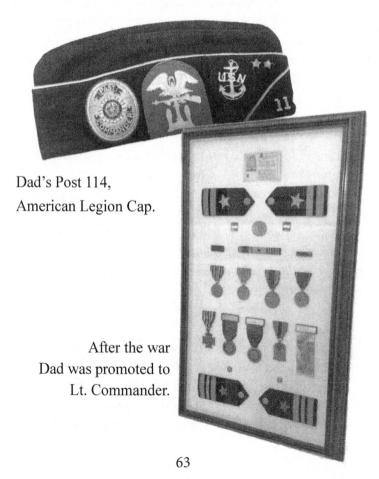

Dad's Post 114,
American Legion Cap.

After the war
Dad was promoted to
Lt. Commander.

Here is one speech he made to a school class on what the American Flag meant to him on foreign soil:

I am happy to be here this morning at this celebration of the dedication of your school flag on this fine autumn day. Mrs. Moore has asked me to tell you what "My Flag Meant To Me On Foreign Soil" during the last World War. It was my connecting link with my home and if we had not been able to safely carry the flag to the far flung corners of the earth and bring it back, none of us would have our home as we know it today.

I served with the Navy for 40 months. As I look back, one of the proudest moments of those 40 months was when I took command of my ship and placed her in Commission. With my wife watching the ceremony, we stood at attention and "Old Glory" was run up the gaff on the main mast. Here now was a ship, no longer merely a mass of gray steel, but almost a living breathing thing, that had the personality of the men aboard her and she was to be our home for the next year. Where we were going we did not know, but we soon had orders to report to Coco Solo, Canal Zone. We were on the high seas for almost a week. Old Glory was above us and we were a part of the U.S.A. Our first stop on foreign soil was in Panama ... a friendly nation. There they flew our flag alongside their own. Everyone had admiration for us, our flag and our country. We were protecting them as well as ourselves.

As I look back, one of the prettiest sights that I remember was Christmas Morning, 1944. We were in Pearl Harbor. Its slopes were palm fringed and in the background were the mountains. A great fleet had been assembled in Pearl Harbor for the assault that was to come soon on one of the Japanese possessions. But we were a far ways from war that Christmas morning. The soft sunlight was shining, and from the mainmast of each ship, holiday size colors were flying in the gentle breeze. In less than two months these majestic ships were to again become the forces of destruction that were to shell to rubble the Japanese fortifications on Iwo Jima and cover our brave Marines when they landed on the hostile beach. And I remember our flag flying over the fleet as it entered, Eniwetok, taken from the Japanese only a year before, while we refueled and provisioned... and a week later I remember our flag as we held battle rehearsals at Saipan and Tinian taken from the Japanese six months before... and then we received the message. This is it. Proceed to attack Iwo Jima. Every man knows his duty. I am confident he will do it and remember the Japanese radio telling us in English not to attack Iwo Jima because we would only die... and the flag moved steadily and unrelentlessly on... on to the inferno that was to be Iwo Jima, the hottest battle in the Pacific. I remember those brave men who first took our flag ashore at Iwo Jima. I remember those brave men who fought their way to the top of Mt. Suribachi and placed our flag there. That flag-raising became a symbol of bravery throughout our country and many of you probably remember seeing the pictures of it. I remember the Japanese radio telling us that while the Stars and Stripes had flown there temporarily, now the "Rising Sun" flag was back again... and through the smoke of battle I strained my eyes and could see "Old Glory" waving in the breeze, from the top of the mountain.

...and then I went ashore. After the fury of the battle was over, after the Island had been secured they raised a flag pole. Admiral Nimitz, Commander of the Pacific Ocean Areas, was coming to take command of the island for the Government of the United States. The bugles

blew "attention". The Admiral walked to the flag pole. The bugles sounded "Colors". A large American flag was "broke out" and smartly raised to the top of the pole. We stood at rigid salute and followed "Old Glory" to the top of the pole with our eyes. There has never been a more stirring emotion in my life than when I stood there and thought of the men who had given their lives for the flag to be raised there, when I thought of the mean who lived thru the ordeal and who would return home and take up their peacetime pursuits and live for the flag. "The Star Spangled Banner, long may it wave, over the land of the free and the home of the brave."

Dad loved America almost as much as he loved Pawleys Island. He spent many of his summers growing up on Pawleys Island. His Grandfather Black, a confederate veteran, taught Dad his love for fishing.

One of the first things he did after his return from the war was to purchase a lot on Pawleys Island. Shortly thereafter a house was built, the same house where I spent my teenaged summers. A wooden boat and 5-horse Johnson outboard motor were also acquired for off-shore fishing. Even later in life, Dad could be seen catching more than his share of flounder and plugging for winter trout in the Pawley's Creek. He had a reputation of being one of the best fishermen in the area. He also built a boat rental business on the Pawley's Creek known as "Bill's Boats". The building and boats were all painted orange. I ran "Bill's Boats" the first two summers until I went to college in September 1953. Today the boat house is a favorite subject for artists.

Dad had always had an interest in teaching, and with my Mother's approval, he went back to college to take several education courses he needed to acquire a teaching certificate. He taught world history and also served as Assistant High School Principal of Winyah High School.

Here are several comments made by some of Dad's former students:

Memories of Winyah High School 1964 – 1968 by Carter Joseph

Perhaps the most memorable teacher from freshman year was Mr. William Walter (WW) Doar, a grizzled World War Two veteran who taught world history and brooked no nonsense from us teenagers. He was a great teacher, and master of his class. If you cut up in any way, BAM! – you were sent to Mr. Rice's office. But beneath that gruff exterior was a gruff interior. He was tough but fair, and he knew what he was talking about. More importantly, he knew how to get you through his class. If you failed, that was your own stupid fault, because he would let you know well in advance the absolute minimum of what was required. If you just barely passed the course, it meant that you had paid little attention and weren't worth any more of his time. He would always announce when covering a particularly important historical event: "Pay attention now! This question WILL BE ON THE TEST! If you miss this question, YOU WILL FAIL THE COURSE!" If you received an A in this class you deserved it, because it meant that you really broke your neck studying.

The following is a portion of an article written by one of Dad's students that appeared in the Coastal Observer on Thursday, August 15, 2013:

Surf Club Reunion catches a wave of nostalgia
Those were the days. Even cutting school to surf occasionally worked out.
Walker said he and some friends saw an old man casting into the surf on the north end of the island one beautiful, warm day. As they got closer, they realized it was W. W. Doar, vice principal of their high school, playing hooky.
"We were supposed to be in school," Walker said. "So was he. We saw who it was and paddled right by him. 'Mr. Doar, see you taking a day off from school too.'
"We went in the next day and heard the announcement: 'Larry Walker come to the principal's office.' He had me an excused absence. Needless to say we didn't have to worry about missing school as long as we caught him over there at the beach."

Later he became Director of the Head Start Program in Georgetown County. He was instrumental in organizing that program which was very successful.

In retirement, my Mother and Father spent a great deal of their time on Pawleys Island – Dad fishing and Mother reading. They would leave Georgetown in early May after the annual meeting of the Winyah Indigo Society and remain at Pawleys Island until the cold weather drove them back home in November. Dad once told me he believed he was the last person to leave Pawleys Island just before Hurricane Hazel struck the Island in 1954. Hurricanes seemed to excite Dad. Maybe they reminded him of the war.

Dad was a serious person, "a place for everything and everything in its place." Some even found him stern, but he also had a soft spot especially for those for whom he cared.

As further evidence of his tender heart, here is a copy of a letter he wrote me on August 31, 1959 as I was leaving to return to my duty assignment with the U.S. Air Force at Goose Bay Labrador. He was writing from Allendale, S.C. where he had a temporary job as office manager with R. L. Morrison & Sons Construction Co. which was constructing docks on the Savannah River.

Allendale, S.C.
August 31, 1959

Dear Bill:

It was with a heavy heart that I left you at Pawley's this morning, realizing that it will probably be many months before I see you again. Possibly a father's love is not as manifest as a mother's love is, but I am sure that it is just as deep, even for a son.

I know that you are just starting your life and you have every attribute to make yours a happy and fruitful life. I have every confidence in you and I am sure that you will use this tour of duty to improve your ability. I am just sorry that the world is in such a condition that it is necessary for your country to have to take three years out of your life. However, always remember that the U.S. is the best Country in the world and since it is necessary that you serve in the military, I know that you will do a good job of it. May God's blessing always be upon you. If at any time I can help you or do anything for you, all you have to do is let me know and I will do the best that I can.

You have a wonderful wife and we want her to understand that our home is her home whenever she wants to come to it.

Lots of love,
Daddy

As previously stated, Dad was very patriotic. He told me on many occasions the thrill he received when he heard the Star Spangled Banner sung or "Old Glory" being hoisted up the flag pole. He was a prime example of a member of the "Greatest Generation" that won World War II then returned home with vitality to build a strong and enduring America.

Dad had a few good friends but many acquaintances. Former students and business colleagues still tell me what a good teacher and ethical business man he was. He influenced many, including me.

Dad married Julia Poag on November 30, 1929. They met in Florida where Julia was employed as a kindergarten teacher and Dad as a construction worker. Julia survived Dad's death by several years. Both are buried in the Doar family plot at Prince George Winyah Church cemetery.

CPSIA information can be obtained at www.ICGtesting.com
Printed in the USA
BVOW08s0207060815

412132BV00001B/15/P